The Economics of Energy

The Pros and Cons of Wind Power

B. J. Best

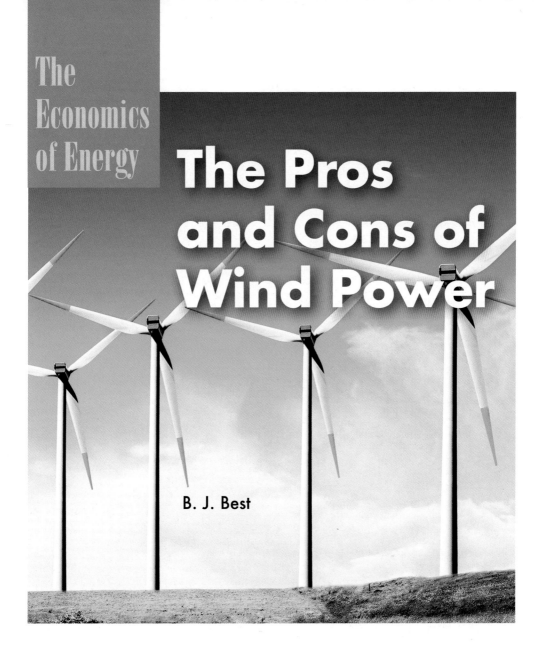

Cavendish
Square
New York

Published in 2016 by Cavendish Square Publishing, LLC
243 5th Avenue, Suite 136, New York, NY 10016

Library of Congress Cataloging-in-Publication Data

Best, B. J., 1976-
The pros and cons of wind power / B.J. Best.
pages cm. — (The economics of energy)
Includes index.
ISBN 978-1-5026-0952-6 (hardcover) ISBN 978-1-5026-0953-3 (ebook)
1. Wind power. 2. Wind turbines. 3. Renewable energy sources. I. Title.

TJ828.B47 2016
333.9'2—dc23

2015032969

Editorial Director: David McNamara
Editor: Amy Hayes/Ryan Nagelhout
Copy Editor: Nathan Heidelberger
Art Director: Jeffrey Talbot

Designer: Amy Greenan
Production Manager: Jennifer Ryder-Talbot
Production Editor: Renni Johnson
Photo Researcher: J8 Media

Printed in the United States of America

Table of Contents

5 Chapter 1
The Work of Wind

29 Chapter 2
**The Advantages of
Wind Power**

45 Chapter 3
**The Disadvantages of
Wind Power**

63 Chapter 4
**The Future of
Wind Power**

73 Glossary

75 Find Out More

78 Index

80 About the Author

All around the world, wind is constantly doing work. Wind is frequently stronger on ocean shorelines.

Chapter 1

The Work of Wind

Perhaps you've driven by an old, broken windmill on a farm. Maybe you live near modern wind turbines that use wind to generate electricity. If you've ever blown into a pinwheel or gone sailing, you've seen how air, the invisible gas all around us, can do work.

What Is Wind?

Earth's atmosphere is constantly moving, and our air circulates around the globe. We experience this movement of air as wind. Wind blows because of two main sources: the sun and the Earth's rotation.

Wind flows from areas of high pressure to areas of low pressure. The sun constantly heats the Earth, and it changes the pressure of the air. Warm air rises, and it leaves behind an area of low pressure beneath it. Cooler air from an area of high pressure then blows in along the surface to fill the area of low pressure. This creates wind on Earth's surface.

Since the Earth is shaped like a sphere, the equatorial regions of Earth receive the most heat because they are directly under the sun for most of the year. Earth's poles, in contrast, receive only glancing rays from the sun, and only during certain times of the year. This causes the air at the equator to become hot and rise. Cooler air will then blow in, causing a steady flow of wind into the equator.

However, Earth rotates from west to east. This rotation influences both the air and water on our planet—they swirl as Earth rotates. Generally speaking, wind in the Northern Hemisphere tends to curl to the right (clockwise), while wind in the Southern Hemisphere curls to the left (counterclockwise). This is known as the **Coriolis effect**, which impacts ocean currents in a similar way.

The air that rises from the equator sinks at around thirty degrees latitude. This cooler air comes into the equator from the east because of the planet's rotation. However, if you live in the Northern Hemisphere, the wind comes from the northeast because of the Coriolis effect. In the Southern Hemisphere, the wind comes from the southeast. These winds are known as the trade winds. They are reliable winds that were very important for ships that sailed trade routes across the sea. Directly on the equator, there is very little wind because that is where the Earth is hottest and most air is moving straight up.

Another band of wind between thirty and sixty degrees latitude is known as the westerlies. This area of atmosphere is separated from the tropics, and generates its own weather patterns. Again, because of the Earth's rotation, wind in the Northern Hemisphere generally blows from the southwest, while it comes from the northwest in the Southern Hemisphere. Finally, at sixty degrees latitude and above, the cold polar air tends to swirl to the east. Each of these wind bands—at the equator, thirty degrees, and sixty degrees—are separated by high-pressure

This illustration shows the range of westerlies around the world. They blow between 30 and 60 degrees latitude.

areas where the winds are usually light, keeping the bands somewhat independent of each other.

However, wind does not always blow in the same direction. Weather and geography can greatly impact wind direction and speed. In addition to global wind patterns, there are many smaller regions of high and low pressure. High pressure usually means clear, sunny days with light

A DEEPER DIVE

How the Land Shapes the Wind

Geographic features also can impact the wind. The coasts of oceans, seas, and large lakes are often windy places. This is because water changes temperature more slowly than land. During the day, as the sun heats the land, the air over the land rises. Cooler air from the body of water then comes in to replace it. This is known as a sea breeze. Then, at night, the process reverses. With no sun, the land cools off more quickly than water. Cooler air sinks, and the wind blows out toward the body of water.

A similar process happens in mountainous areas. During the day, the sun heats land in valleys and low-lying areas. This air blows up the side of the mountain, and cooler air descends from a higher altitude. At night, cooler air sweeps down the side of the mountain into low areas, as the last of their warm air rises into the atmosphere. Of course, because mountains are much higher than other places on Earth, they are frequently windier year-round. The highest wind speed not from a tornado ever recorded in the continental United States was atop Mt. Washington in New Hampshire: 231 miles per hour (372 kilometers per hour)!

winds. Low pressure can mean windy days as air rushes in to fill the low pressure. Low pressure systems often have warm and cool air conflicting, which can result in storms. In the Northern Hemisphere, a low-pressure system will have winds swirl around it counterclockwise because of the Coriolis effect. Air doesn't move straight to the area of lowest pressure. Likewise, winds swirl clockwise away from a high-pressure area in the Northern Hemisphere. These pressure systems often determine the direction of wind in a particular location.

Catching the Wind

The earliest known use of wind to perform work for humans is sailing. Sailboats are thought to have been invented in Egypt around 3200 BCE. Before sailboats existed, large boats could only be moved in two ways. They could move with the current of a river, which only permitted travel in one direction. They could also be rowed, often by slaves. The Egyptians needed an efficient way to travel along the Nile River. The earliest sailboats had one square sail. The boat could only sail in the direction the wind was blowing. Fortunately, the wind along the Nile typically blows upstream. The earliest sailors could sail upstream, then let the river's current carry them back downstream.

By 1500 BCE, the Egyptians had developed their river boats into ships that could sail long distances on seas. Triangle-shaped sails, which allowed a sailboat to sail in many different directions, were in use in the Mediterranean Sea as early as the second century BCE. Sea trade routes were well established and very important for the Roman Empire. From there, as sails became more effective, ships became bigger and faster.

Egyptians used boats such as these to sail up the Nile River. The river's currents would carry them back downstream.

Ships allowed for the Age of Discovery. This was a time of European exploration and settlement between the fifteenth and eighteenth centuries. Europeans visited North America, South America, and Asia. Ships also became tools of war. Both ancient Greece and the Roman Empire had large navies that helped expand their territories. The Netherlands, Great Britain, and Spain also had powerful navies in the seventeenth and eighteenth centuries.

A DEEPER DIVE

The Fastest Sailboats and Their Decline

In the middle of the nineteenth century, some of the fastest sailing ships were built. These were known as clippers. They were huge boats that could have twenty sails or more. The fastest clippers sailed at an average speed of about 18 miles per hour (29 kmh). They were used for trade and transportation. However, steamships were quickly becoming popular as a faster and more reliable mode of transportation. The use of sailboats quickly declined. Still, many people continue to use sailboats today for travel and sport, continuing a human activity of more than five thousand years.

A Timeline of Wind Power Use

3200 BCE Egyptians invent the sailboat

200 BCE–**800** CE Windmills are invented in Persia and China

1414 The first recorded use of a windmill in the Netherlands

1832 Michael Faraday invents the dynamo

1853 *Flying Cloud*, a clipper ship, sets a world record in sailing from New York to San Francisco in 89 days and 8 hours; the record lasts until 1989

1888 Charles Brush builds the first wind turbine which reliably generates electricity

1902 The first mass-produced cars in the United States are built

1931 The first vertical-axis wind turbine (VAWT) is patented by Georges Jean Marie Darrieus

1941 The first turbine to provide electricity to the US power grid operates in Vermont

1973 The oil crisis restricts access to oil around the globe

1979 A second oil crisis impacts worldwide oil supplies

1980 The world's first wind farm is built in New Hampshire

1980s Construction of the Tehachapi Pass Wind Farm in California, one of the first large wind farms in the United States

1991 The world's first offshore wind farm is built in Denmark

1992 The US offers its first subsidies for wind power

2005 The Kyoto Protocol, an international treaty that requires nations to reduce greenhouse gas emissions, goes into effect; the United States, the world's largest polluter at the time, does not sign the treaty

2009 Construction begins on the Gansu Wind Farm in China, currently the world's largest wind farm in terms of potential power

2010 Construction begins on the Alta Wind Energy Center in California, currently the largest wind farm in the United States

2011 Construction begins on the London Array off the southeast coast of the United Kingdom, currently the world's largest offshore wind farm

The First Windmills

In ancient times, agriculture became an established practice. But growing crops was difficult and took much time. Two major challenges early farmers faced were getting enough water to irrigate their crops, and grinding wheat they grew into flour. These farmers eventually turned to the wind to do some of their work.

The principle behind the windmill is the transfer of energy. Wind has energy because the air is moving. Ancient peoples wondered if they could capture that energy on land the same way people did at sea in their sailboats. If they could collect the wind and transfer it to a machine that could help in their labors, they could be more efficient.

No one is sure when windmills were first invented—estimates range from 200 BCE to 800 CE. People believe windmills began to be used in two separate places: in Persia (now present-day Iran) and in China. Farmers in both of these places needed to get water and grind grain. The earliest windmills in Persia were built with cloth sails lashed to a framework of reeds. These sails were attached to a vertical pole. When the wind blew hard enough, the sails would rotate parallel to the ground and do mechanical work. Some windmills were attached to pumps that drew water from lakes or rivers, or from a hole dug in the earth. Other windmills turned a giant round stone, the **millstone**, which would grind grain into flour.

In early history, people had harnessed water to do some of this work. As early as 300 BCE, Greeks channeled water flowing from a river over a large wheel. The water turned the wheel, which then turned a millstone inside a mill. A mill powered by water is called a watermill. Soon, people were using the energy of water to perform other labors, including crushing stone and sawing lumber.

However, rivers and streams only exist in certain places. Someone who wished to grind wheat but lived far away from a watermill had to do it by hand, a difficult task. On the other hand, wind is everywhere on Earth. European traders who had been to Persia and the Middle East told stories of how effective the windmills were, and farmers began building them in Europe in the twelfth century CE.

The windmill was an especially important invention for European farmers. The nobility and the clergy of Europe controlled the locations of watermills, as well as the rights to use them. By building a windmill, a farmer was giving himself the opportunity to make a living on his own.

"The Dutch Built Holland"

The Netherlands is a country in northern Europe, west of Germany. The country's name literally means "low country." About half of the country lies 3 feet (1 meter) above sea level or lower, while one-eighth of the country is below sea level. As a result, the land was prone to constant flooding from the sea as well as its major rivers. The earliest attempts to control floods were manmade dikes. Dikes are long banks of earth and wood that serve as a barrier between water and land. These proved successful and allowed easier settling of the Netherlands with less fear of towns being destroyed by floods.

As the country continued to expand in the Middle Ages, people needed more places to live. Dutch people began to reclaim flooded land that was below sea level. At first, they used men and horses to drain and

The Netherlands is known for its beautiful windmills. This photo is from about 1905.

The Pros and Cons of Wind Power

move water. But as the windmill became more popular in Europe, the Dutch saw that they could use the windmill to do much of this work. The earliest recorded use of a windmill to pump water in the Netherlands was in 1414. From there, the use of windmills quickly expanded. This allowed the Dutch to create many polders. A polder is a piece of land below sea level completely enclosed by dikes and drained by hand or machine. The combination of dikes and windmills allowed the Dutch to settle in these polders. People increased the amount of land available in the country for living and farming.

These windmills were hollow-post mills and had four blades made with wood in a lattice pattern. Sometimes sails were stretched across this framework. These blades could then be rotated around the center post to allow them to catch the most wind. When the wind blew, it turned the blades of the mill, which then turned a scoop wheel. The scoop wheel would collect water from a lower area and then raise it to a higher area, where it was dumped.

A few of these windmills are still in use today for water drainage. The windmill became a picturesque symbol for the Netherlands. There is a saying that "the Dutch built Holland" (another name for the Netherlands), and while that applies to many aspects of Dutch culture, it is certainly true for windmills. The Dutch literally created new land through wind power.

Windmills in the Nineteenth Century

By the 1800s, windmill technology had been around for at least one thousand years. Many people still used wind to grind grain and draw water. The windmill was particularly important in the western expansion

Many early farms and ranches in the American West relied on windmills to provide water.

of the United States. As people moved further westward beyond the Mississippi River, they encountered vast prairies and plains. Farmers wished to settle and grow crops, but they weren't always located near a river or other water source. They still needed water for irrigation, feeding livestock, and daily living.

These farmers used windmills. By the nineteenth century, technology had changed to make sturdier, lighter, and more efficient mills. The windmills that dotted the American Midwest and West were made of wood and eventually steel. They were supported by four legs, with a pipe in the middle to draw water. The mills had many blades arranged in a circle.

Behind the blades was a metal tail, known as a **vane**. The vane would keep the blades pointed into the wind in order to catch the most energy.

Windmills eventually fell out of use because of other technological advances, such as internal combustion engines. Many still exist today on rural farms, although they are typically no longer used. Another key technology—electrical power—would also change how people viewed windmills.

Wind into Electricity

For centuries, humans had captured the wind's energy to do other mechanical work. The windmills turned gears that operated simple machinery to pump water or grind grain. But in the late 1800s, inventors began exploring how wind energy could be turned into an entirely different form of energy: electricity.

In 1832, English scientist Michael Faraday discovered that if you spun a copper wheel rapidly near a stationary magnet, you could produce an electromagnetic force. The force could be carried through wires in the form of electricity. Other inventors quickly improved upon his designs. By the middle of the nineteenth century, these electrical generators, known as **dynamos**, could produce a steady and reliable output of electricity.

One of these other inventors was Charles F. Brush from Cleveland, Ohio. Brush developed electric lights. He also developed an efficient dynamo to power them in 1876. The sale of Brush's lights and electrical equipment made him wealthy. He began his own electric company. But electricity at this time was bought by organizations who most needed it—industries, businesses, and the government. Most homes did not have electricity.

A DEEPER DIVE

The Economics of the First Electric Windmill

Brush's windmill was so large and successful that it drew a lot of attention. Many national publications wrote articles about it. Some people thought it was nice to be able to get "free" electricity, since wind costs nothing. However, an 1890 *Scientific American* article warns:

> The reader must not suppose that electric lighting by means of power supplied in this way is cheap because the wind costs nothing. On the contrary, the cost of the plant is so great as to more than offset the cheapness of the motive power. However, there is a great satisfaction in making use of one of nature's most unruly motive agents.

In 1888, Charles Brush built a giant windmill to generate electricity. A man stands in the lower right corner to show the windmill's scale.

Brush thought about using wind to power one of his dynamos. In 1888, he built a huge windmill. Its **rotor**, or spinning blades, was over 50 feet (15 m) across and was comprised of 144 cedar blades. The windmill was 60 feet (18 m) tall and had a tail 60 feet long. The windmill turned one of Brush's dynamos. It charged batteries he kept in his basement laboratory. The windmill reliably powered lights and Brush's other inventions for twenty years. It is the first known use of a windmill to reliably generate electricity.

Power in the Twentieth Century

Wind wasn't the only way people made power. Steam helped fuel the Industrial Revolution in the late eighteenth and early nineteenth centuries. Steam was produced by boiling water with burning coal. The steam was then used to drive an engine. These engines powered machines in factories. They also moved vehicles such as ships and trains. The engines were very efficient. Coal was seen as the most important energy source for the future.

As electrical demand grew, entrepreneurs created power stations. These stations used steam to power large generators. The generators supplied electricity through wires to paying customers. Because they were steam-driven, they required large amounts of coal as well.

At the same time, internal combustion engines were being developed. These engines require an outside fuel, typically made from oil. Oil is refined and used to make gasoline and other fuels to run engines. This type of engine was crucial to the development of the automobile. Automobiles began being mass-produced in the United States in the early 1900s. They became incredibly popular, increasing the demand for fuels produced from oil.

Automobiles with combustion engines, like this one from 1910, quickly became a popular mode of transportation.

With this rapid industrialization, wind power looked old and quaint. Windmills were still being used in rural areas, but by the early twentieth century, people expected machines to be run by motors and electricity. There was no wide-scale adoption of Brush's ideas of wind-powered electricity. Instead, the use of coal and oil spread rapidly during the first half of the twentieth century. Following World War II, Americans enjoyed low fuel prices. They bought large cars. Many people moved from cities to suburbs, which required more driving. The American population was

During the oil crisis of 1973, some gas stations used color-coded systems to let people know if gas was available to buy.

The Pros and Cons of Wind Power

greatly expanding. That caused more demand for electricity for homes, businesses, and government. It appeared that oil and coal would be the future of American power forever. But that would be impossible.

Fossil Fuels and the Oil Crisis of 1973

Coal and oil, along with natural gas, are known as **fossil fuels**. Fossil fuels were formed about three hundred million years ago during a time known as the Carboniferous Period. The Earth was a very swampy place with a warmer climate. Much land at the time was covered in huge plants, such as ferns and trees. As these plants died, they sank to the bottoms of swamps and oceans, where they decomposed. Over millions of years, these remains got buried under silt, mud, clay, and more and more rock. The immense pressure of all of this rock broke the remains down to carbon (which is where the Carboniferous Period gets its name). Depending on the types of plants, this carbon became oil, coal, and natural gas.

In order to access fossil fuels, people need to dig deep in the ground. Coal miners bring coal to the surface from underground, while oil wells are drilled deep and pump oil up. Because the only way to form fossil fuels is millions of years and immense pressure, there is a limited supply. Fossil fuels are called **nonrenewable resources** because there is no way to make more of them. Once they are used up, they are gone.

About half of the world's oil is located in the Middle East. In 1973, a group of countries in the Middle East declared an oil embargo, which meant they would not sell oil to the United States, Canada, Japan, much of Europe, and other countries. At that time, the United States heavily relied on oil for gasoline for their cars, and US oil production was declining.

Prices for oil sharply increased. This led to unusual measures in the United States. Gasoline supplies were rationed, or limited. Only certain people could buy it at certain times. The US speed limit was reduced to 55 mph (89 kmh) in part to reduce gas usage.

The oil crisis raised people's awareness of how we use energy. People didn't always have control over the energy sources they used. Energy supplies could disappear quickly. In response to the crisis, the United States formed the Department of Energy in 1977. The Department of Energy helps manage the nation's energy usage and policies.

People saw how energy from the fossil fuels they used could not last forever. But some energy sources were limitless. After the oil crisis, people began to look more seriously at other ways to generate power. One of them was a source humans had been using for more than five thousand years: wind.

CRITICAL THINKING

- For Egypt, the Roman Empire, and other nations, why did sailboats become important vehicles for trade?

- Why did demand for electricity grow during the nineteenth and twentieth centuries?

- In the twentieth century, why did businesses and consumers behave as if fossil fuels would never run out?

These workers are looking at blueprints for wind turbines. The number of turbines built around the world increases every year.

Chapter 2

The Advantages of Wind Power

The industrialized world has been powered by fossil fuels for over a century. When these fuels became heavily used, no one thought of problems they might cause. People were looking for cheap, effective sources of power. However, the enormous use of fossil fuels caused much damage.

Since fossil fuels are nonrenewable, they will be used up. No one is sure when our supplies of oil, coal, and natural gas will disappear. Some believe these resources will be almost completely gone by the end of this century. If businesses and consumers continue to use only fossil fuels, there will be a point where they will no longer have power.

The Problems with Fossil Fuels

Fossil fuels also cause another worldwide problem: pollution. The only way to use fossil fuels is to burn them. The smoke released from burning fossil fuels pollutes cities and creates smog. This pollution has greatly impacted **global warming**, also known as climate change.

A DEEPER DIVE

Supply and Demand

As the reserves of fossil fuels shrink, the cost of them will rise. This is because of an economic model known as supply and demand. The model says if there is a large demand for a product, the price will be higher. The model also says if a market has a large supply of a product, its price will be low. As the quantity of fossil fuels shrinks, so will the supply. Yet the demand will still be very strong. People will need coal to fuel power plants and oil to make gasoline for engines. Therefore, prices will rise. If many people still need power from fossil fuels but there is very little supply left, the prices will be incredibly high around the world. Only the richest and most powerful companies and people will be able to afford the power they need.

Dangerous pollution is a major result of coal-burning power plants. The pollution causes global warming and health issues for people living nearby.

Burning fossil fuels releases gases into the air, primarily carbon dioxide (CO_2). Carbon dioxide is a **greenhouse gas**. Greenhouse gases rise into the Earth's atmosphere and become trapped there. They act like a greenhouse around the Earth. They let heat in but are slow to let it out. Human activity, led by the use of fossil fuels, has increased the average temperature of our planet by 1.4 degrees Fahrenheit (0.77 degrees Celsius) over the past one hundred years. This might seem like a small change, but even small temperature changes can have disastrous effects.

There are many environmental hazards associated with global warming. Polar ice caps are melting, raising sea levels. This endangers wildlife, such as polar bears, which live on the ice caps. It also increases flooding risks for coastal cities. Global warming also makes weather patterns more extreme. This can lead to severe droughts, which impact water supplies and agriculture. These dry conditions also bring more wildfires. Global warming can cause heavier rainstorms, resulting in dangerous flooding. Eventually, it will also cause stronger storms such as hurricanes.

Despite evidence clearly showing how global warming is damaging our planet, many people continue to use fossil fuels without concern. Earth's average temperature is expected to rise somewhere between 2°F and 11°F (1.1°C and 6°C) over the next hundred years. This will make worldwide environmental problems worse.

In the United States in 2014, 67 percent of all electricity was generated from fossil fuels. The many problems with fossil fuels have driven people to look for other energy sources. Is there an energy source that is plentiful, inexpensive, and clean? Some people believe wind is the answer.

A Modern Wind Turbine

Modern wind turbines—the contemporary name for windmills that produce electricity—look very different than windmills from the past. Engineers have created turbines that use wind more efficiently. The most common type of industrial wind turbine has three blades, each more than 100 feet (30 m) long. They are placed atop a tall tower more than 200 feet (61 m) high. The blades spin because of the scientific principle of lift. They are shaped similarly to the wings of an airplane. The blades need to be lightweight but very strong. They are typically made of advanced materials, such as carbon fiber. Together, these blades are known as the rotor.

The rotor is connected to the **nacelle**. A nacelle is a box that sits atop the turbine's tower that contains the components to turn the rotor's motion into electricity. As the rotor turns, it spins gears in a gear box. The gear box takes the slow revolutions of the rotor and increases them to a speed

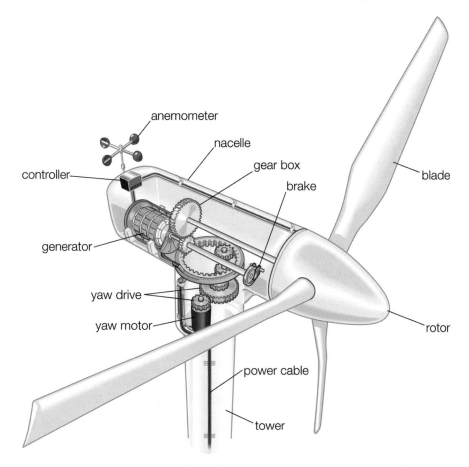

anemometer

nacelle

gear box

controller

brake

blade

generator

yaw drive

yaw motor

rotor

power cable

tower

This diagram shows the key parts that allow a wind turbine to generate electricity.

that can turn a generator. The generator creates electricity in the same way as earlier dynamos. The electricity flows through cables down the inside of the tower, then to outside cables.

The nacelle has other key components. Since the turbine is most effective when its blades are pointed directly into the wind, many nacelles have a wind vane on top of them. Information from the vane is fed to a computer. This computer operates motors to change the rotor's direction, or yaw, so the blades face the wind. Also inside the nacelle is a braking system that can help slow down or stop the rotor in very high winds or for maintenance.

Today's Use of Wind

The electricity produced by wind turbines is measured in **kilowatt-hours**, abbreviated kWh. One kilowatt-hour is enough electricity to power a microwave for about an hour, or an LCD TV for about five hours. The average American home uses about 900 kilowatt-hours a month. How much electricity an individual turbine produces depends on many factors. These factors include size, power capacity, and wind speed. But generally, a new wind turbine can be expected to generate up to 4,700 **megawatt-hours** (4,700 MWh, or 4.7 million kWh) of electricity per year.

The grid is the network of power lines that delivers power to people who need it. It includes the wires and transformers that move power over long distances.

The electricity from a wind turbine is connected via cables to other power lines. These power lines serve the general community and are known as the **grid**. The grid carries electricity generated from different power plants to communities. If you live near more than one type of power plant, there's no way to tell which electricity you're using. Electricity is the same no matter what source was used to create it.

Usually an electric company will not build just one wind turbine in a location. It's expensive to lay cables for one turbine to connect it to the grid. Engineers carefully study areas where winds are strong and reliable. They make maps of average wind speeds. They study the local geography, including hills, bodies of water, buildings, and roads. When a suitable site is determined, companies will build a **wind farm**—a collection of many wind turbines in a close area. The turbines in a wind farm are often placed in rows, carefully spaced to ensure efficient operation.

After a century of fossil fuel use, why are people using more wind power? Supporters give four important reasons.

Wind Is Abundant

Wind energy, along with other alternative energy sources such as solar power and geothermal power, is a **renewable resource**. No matter how much wind a turbine uses to generate electricity, there will always be more. We can never run out of wind on our planet. Compare this to fossil fuels, which have a limited supply.

Wind is also everywhere on this planet. No matter where you are, the air is always moving. That means any location on Earth has some energy that could be harnessed. Of course, many parts of the world do not have strong or sufficiently reliable winds. Still, unlike fossil fuels, all countries are rich in wind.

Finally, wind is free. It is natural energy, which costs nothing. Fossil fuel prices fluctuate according to supply and demand but will only increase in the long-term. No one can charge for access to the wind.

A DEEPER DIVE

Today's Wind around the World

Some of the earliest wind farms in the United States were located in California. The largest wind farm in the country is still located there. However, not all wind farms are on land. Wind is usually stronger over the ocean. More than fifty offshore wind farms have been built in Europe. The largest is the London Array, off the southeast coast of the United Kingdom. The London Array has 175 turbines and can produce enough electricity to power more than 470,000 homes.

There are more than 200,000 industrial wind turbines around the world. They are capable of producing about 370,000 megawatts (mW) of power. The amount of wind power available has increased by about 15 percent over each of the past several years. China has also made large investments in wind power and is the world leader in wind power capacity. The United States is the world's largest producer of wind energy, though, generating 141 terawatt-hours of electricity in 2012—that's 141 billion kilowatt-hours!

The London Array is the world's largest offshore wind farm. It generates enough electricity to power a city about the size of Kansas City, Missouri.

However, China and the United States are large countries, and neither generates much of its total energy supply from wind. In the United States, wind energy accounts for about 4 percent of the nation's overall usage. Many European countries have been committed to wind energy for much longer. In fact, Spain, Portugal, Ireland, the United Kingdom, and Germany each generate more than 10 percent of their countries' energy needs from wind. Denmark uses wind power for 28 percent of its energy needs.

Wind Is Clean

Compared to the pollution and global warming caused by using fossil fuels, wind is a very clean power source. Wind does not get dirtier by blowing through a turbine's rotor. It does not contain any additional harmful chemicals. A coal-fueled power plant constantly sends up large plumes of carbon dioxide and other toxic gases. The burning of fossil fuels for energy is the world's largest contributor to global warming.

Unlike wind energy, smokestacks from coal power plants release smoke and pollution into the air.

Nuclear power plants don't create greenhouse gases, but they can create other environmental hazards. Nuclear power plants split uranium atoms to create heat. This heat then boils water to make steam. The steam drives generators to make electricity. But this process creates radioactive wastes that need to be very carefully stored and disposed. Failure to do so can destroy the surrounding environment.

Wind's clean benefits aren't limited to just generating power. Coal must be constantly mined in order to fuel power plants. This mining requires equipment with engines that burn fossil fuels. Methane, a powerful greenhouse gas, is often vented out of mines and released into the atmosphere. The coal must then be transported to the power plants. This also requires vehicles that burn fossil fuels. Uranium must similarly be mined and transported.

Traditional power plants—both coal and nuclear—can harm their local environment. Power plants use large quantities of water. If a plant is drawing water from a local water source, it could impact the plant and animal life in that water. As the water is used in the plant, it becomes contaminated. This water must be carefully disposed of and cleaned before it is safe. If it is released into the environment, it can damage the ecosystem.

Many people consider pollution and global warming to be the most pressing problem our planet faces. Using more wind energy will help slow the dangerous impacts of our dependence on fossil fuels.

Workers who service wind turbines take care to be very safe when they are on them.

Wind Is Safe

There are a few risks with operating a wind turbine. A blade could fail: it can be flung from the turbine, potentially injuring a person or destroying a building. In one case, a broken blade traveled a mile from its tower. Other potential hazards include fires in the nacelle. The tower could fail, resulting in its collapse.

While all of these are possibilities, there have only been 161 recorded deaths

A DEEPER DIVE

A Nuclear Disaster

Like wind power, nuclear power is normally very safe, with very few deaths occurring in the United States over the history of its use. However, when nuclear reactors fail, the consequences can be devastating.

In 1986, part of the Chernobyl nuclear power plant in Ukraine exploded. It released huge quantities of radioactive particles into the air. Thirty-one people died immediately as part of the explosion. But exposure to radioactive materials greatly increases the risk of developing cancer. It is difficult to determine how many people will die to exposure to radiation, but the United Nations estimates it will be at least four thousand. Beyond the loss of human life, the explosion at Chernobyl devastated the landscape. The government established a large area around the plant where to this day people are prohibited from living and even visiting.

around the world from wind power as of June 2015. That's a small number over the long history of turbines. Many of these accidents were workers falling from the tower.

Compare this to a coal power plant. In the United States, it is estimated that at least 7,500 people die from pollution from coal every year. In China, which has fewer laws about power plant emissions, 670,000 people a year die from coal pollution.

Wind power has little risk of harming people. Many people believe wind is one of the safest power sources available.

Wind Is Cost Effective

Wind power was expensive in the 1970s and 1980s. Wind turbines couldn't generate much electricity. They were expensive to build. It was also expensive to connect new wind turbines to the existing grid. These costs made people reluctant to invest in wind energy. They didn't see it as an economic alternative to coal-fueled power plants.

However, the technology to build wind turbines rapidly improved. Today's wind turbines are stronger, lighter, and taller than before. They are also capable of generating more power from the same amount of wind. This has made wind power economically attractive.

Energy sources can be compared based on how much it costs to generate a certain amount of electricity. Economists use the **levelized cost of electricity** (LCOE) to measure this cost. The LCOE considers the costs to build a power source, maintain it, and supply it with fuel over the course of its life. The LCOE measures the cost of electricity per kilowatt-hour or megawatt-hour.

Trains often move large blades to sites where new turbines will be built.

In 2015, the US Energy Information Administration (EIA) released a forecast of LCOEs for power plants that would be put into service in 2020. It forecasts that a conventional coal-fueled power plant will have a cost of $95.10 for each MWh of electricity generated. A nuclear power plant's cost is very similar, at $95.20 per MWh. A wind farm on land, by contrast, will produce electricity at the significantly lower rate of $73.60 per MWh. In fact, the EIA forecast says electricity from wind will be cheaper than almost all other sources of power!

Why will wind be so cheap? The biggest reason is that a wind farm doesn't have to pay for its fuel. Wind is free. If coal and natural gas power plants didn't have to pay for fuel, they would be cheaper than wind turbines. But there is no way for those plants to run without the fuel they need.

These four reasons—wind is abundant, wind is clean, wind is safe, and wind is cost effective—make many people excited to support wind power. It makes sense to them environmentally and economically. Yet, there are a variety of concerns with wind turbines. The choice to support wind power might not be as clear as it seems.

CRITICAL THINKING

- How has supply and demand impacted the cost of wind power over time?

- Human-caused global warming is accepted as a fact by almost all credible scientists. But many people still don't believe it's happening. Why?

- One of the advantages of wind is that it is found everywhere. Does that mean we should try to use wind power everywhere?

Although there are many advantages to wind power, there are many unanswered questions about their safety and sustainability.

The Disadvantages of Wind Power

Supporters of wind turbines believe clean, renewable energy will power our future. But not everyone believes wind is the best source for the world's energy needs. These people have several questions to ask supporters of wind power.

Is Wind Power Reliable?

No matter where you live, the wind doesn't blow all the time. Wind speeds change throughout the day. They typically get lower at night. And there are times when there is no wind at all.

Generally, industrial turbines require an average wind speed of 13 miles per hour (21 kilometers per hour, or 6 meters per second). However, the wind doesn't need to be at that speed on the ground. Remember that wind turbines are atop tall towers. Scientists have mapped average wind speeds at about 260 feet (80 m) above the ground. They produce maps, such as the one on the next page, that show where there are good wind resources.

This map of the United States shows that the greatest wind resources are generally located in the central United States. These regions include

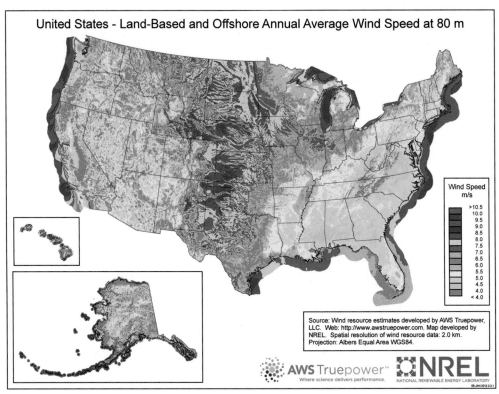

United States - Land-Based and Offshore Annual Average Wind Speed at 80 m

Wind Speed
m/s

>10.5
10.0
9.5
9.0
8.5
8.0
7.5
7.0
6.5
6.0
5.5
5.0
4.5
4.0
< 4.0

Source: Wind resource estimates developed by AWS Truepower, LLC. Web: http://www.awstruepower.com. Map developed by NREL. Spatial resolution of wind resource data: 2.0 km. Projection: Albers Equal Area WGS84.

AWS Truepower™
Where science delivers performance.

NREL
NATIONAL RENEWABLE ENERGY LABORATORY

This map shows where the wind resources in the United States are strongest. Pinks, purples, and blues indicate a high average wind speed.

the Great Plains and the Midwest. As a result, both Iowa and South Dakota currently produce more than 25 percent of their electricity from wind!

Good wind speed is important to effective turbines. The energy of wind is proportional to the cube (or third power) of its speed. This means a small increase in wind speed creates significantly more energy. For example, if the wind speed increases from 10 miles per hour (16 kmh) to 12.6 mph (20 kmh), the available energy in the wind doubles.

However, it is true that wind speeds can vary, even in typically windy areas. Wind turbines can never be in constant use. Critics of wind power

A DEEPER DIVE

Wind and Demand Move Together

Supporters of wind power say wind speeds tend to vary on the same schedule as energy needs. For example, people need more electricity during the day. Businesses and schools are open, and they use a lot of power. Winds tend to decrease at night. Fortunately, that is when people use less power. Businesses are closed, and people are asleep. Wind speeds also vary with the seasons. Winds tend to be stronger in the winter. This is also when people need more power. There are fewer hours of daylight, so people use lights more. The weather is also colder, so people use electricity to heat their homes and businesses.

compare this to coal-fueled power plants, which can operate constantly. Companies that build wind turbines know this. They do extensive surveying of proposed building sites to ensure the best possible wind speed. Building wind farms rather than a single turbine also helps capture as much wind as possible.

Critics of wind power also say that wind speed is not the same everywhere. The wind speed map for the United States shows this. Electricity is produced and used on a local and regional level. Looking at the map, you can see that the many places in the eastern United States do not have high wind resources. A wind turbine built in Nebraska will not provide electricity to someone in Georgia. Those two states are simply too far away. Other renewable energy sources, such as solar or geothermal power, might be better choices in areas with not enough wind.

Do Wind Turbines Ruin the Landscape?

Wind turbines are highly visible. They rise high above the surrounding land where they are built. The rotor is massive. Currently, the largest blades for a wind turbine are 246 feet (75 m) long. Turbines are most commonly painted a uniform white or gray. These contrast strongly with blue sky and green vegetation. A wind farm makes surrounding buildings and roads look tiny. People are not used to seeing such giant structures in rural places. Are wind turbines ugly?

Some people say yes. They believe wind turbines look unnatural and imposing. Outside of cities, we expect to look at a natural landscape and see nothing taller than trees. Wind turbines rise like needles above everything. Critics claim that wind turbines spoil the natural beauty of a landscape.

People must consider how potential windmills would change the views of the surrounding landscape.

Supporters of turbines say that humans have already drastically changed the landscape. Land had to be deforested for farms to be built, for example. Utility poles are unnatural, yet we have become used to them in our natural landscape. People who favor wind turbines claim that as wind power becomes more common, we will accept turbines as part of the landscape as well.

Supporters also point out how our current power plants look. Both nuclear and coal power plants are tall, and they send out large clouds from smokestacks. Nuclear power plants release steam. Coal power plants release smoke, which contains pollution. People who favor wind do not think these methods of generating power are more visually attractive.

Some people protest against building wind turbines due to their disadvantages.

People who live near wind turbines would be most affected, as they see the turbines every day. If turbines were truly ugly, they might decrease property values. People might not want to buy a house near a wind turbine if they considered it ugly. Researchers have conducted many studies on this topic. Most conclude that being able to see wind turbines from a piece of property does not affect its value. This suggests it usually doesn't matter if a turbine is nearby.

Do Wind Turbines Threaten Animals?

Wind turbines are large, unnatural structures typically built in rural areas. Were a wind turbine to be built, local wildlife might be completely unfamiliar with it. Do wind turbines affect animals?

On the ground, most people agree building a wind turbine doesn't have a large impact. The base of the tower is about the same size as a typical house. To many animals on the ground, a wind turbine is just another building. There are problems with animals that fly, though. Wind turbines impact birds and bats.

Scientists say about three hundred thousand birds in the United States die every year due to colliding with wind turbines.

Wind turbines can and do kill birds and bats. The tips of the blades on a turbine can move at 140 miles per hour (225 kmh) or faster. Currently, in the United States, researchers estimate about 300,000 birds die every year from collisions with turbines. However, supporters of wind power say that turbines kill significantly fewer birds every year than vehicles, buildings and windows, and cats. As the number of wind turbines increase, though, so will the number of bird deaths.

Bat deaths could be considered a larger problem. In the United States, scientists estimate about 450,000 bats die every year from wind turbines. Bats might view turbines as very large trees. They could see turbines as a place to roost. Insects often land on the turbines, which provide food for the bats.

Research in the area of animal deaths is incomplete. Results are sometimes contradictory. However, researchers continue to look for ways to reduce fatalities. For example, one study suggests that painting wind turbines purple would help save bats. Insects are less drawn to purple, which might mean bats would be less attracted as well. Careful

A DEEPER DIVE

Choosing Wildlife Over Wind

One example of how a company that creates wind farms takes wildlife into consideration is the London Array. It is the world's largest offshore wind farm, but it was originally planned to be even larger, with an additional 166 turbines. An environmental group was concerned about the turbines' impact on bird populations. They were particularly concerned about red-throated divers, a type of loon. At least one third of the United Kingdom's population of these divers migrates to waters around the London Array. The builders of the array didn't feel they had enough time to prove that additional turbines wouldn't hurt these birds. Therefore, they abandoned plans to build the additional turbines.

Researchers say bats are particularly impacted by wind turbines, with more than 450,000 killed by them each year.

planning of where to locate wind turbines is also important. Wind turbines are recommended to not be located in migration routes for birds and bats, for example.

Animal deaths are an important concern. However, supporters of wind power point to the larger picture. Pollution, acid rain, global warming, and other problems caused by burning fossil fuels are damaging all animals— and people, too. Compared to fossil fuels, wind energy is significantly less destructive to wildlife and habitats.

Do Wind Turbines Threaten Humans?

Some people claim if you live near a wind turbine, it can damage your health. One frequent complaint about turbines is their noise. The wind moving the rotor, along with the rotor slicing through a broad circle of air, results in noisy operation. If people are exposed to too much noise, they can have difficulty sleeping, and it can affect their mental health.

Decibels (dB) are used to measure volume. If you were on top of a wind turbine, the noise would be 105 dB, about the same loudness as a

Some people claim that living or working near a wind turbine can damage your health. Currently, there is little evidence to support this.

lawnmower. However, most regulations require wind turbines to be set 1,000 feet (300 m) away from any home. At that distance, the volume is 43 dB. This is slightly louder than a running refrigerator, and equivalent to the background noise of a library. Supporters of turbines argue the noise is no greater than general background noise found in most cities and towns.

Wind turbines also can generate infrasound. Infrasound is sound below the frequency of human hearing. Since people can't hear infrasound, they might not notice they are being affected by it. Yet infrasound can cause headaches, dizziness, and sleep problems. Some people group these conditions into something called "wind turbine syndrome." These people believe wind turbines cause illnesses. Therefore, turbines shouldn't be built.

There is very little evidence to support that wind turbine syndrome exists. While turbines create infrasound, no one has proved a direct link to illness. Some people have sued builders of wind farms. Almost all of these cases have been dismissed. Courts around the world do not believe there is enough evidence to prove that turbines cause health problems. In 2015, the National Health and Medical Research Council of Australia said, "There is currently no consistent evidence that wind farms cause adverse health effects in humans." However, the council also recommended further research in the area. As more turbines are built, research is likely to continue. People want to know if there are health risks from living near wind power facilities.

Are Wind Turbines Expensive?

In order to begin providing wind power, a company must spend a lot of money. Costs vary depending on the type of turbine built, but most industrial turbines cost at least $1.3 million. Therefore, a wind farm of twenty turbines would cost at least $26 million! Overall, though, according to the US Energy Information Administration (EIA), in 2020 the cost per megawatt-hour to build wind turbines will be similar to building a coal power plant.

These costs only include construction. It also costs money to integrate electricity from turbines into the existing grid. Cables are usually buried from a wind farm and lead to a substation. The substation collects the electricity produced from all the turbines on a wind farm. It then provides that electricity to the general power grid.

In some cases, the existing grid might not be big enough to support new producers of electricity. Additional power lines might be needed.

A DEEPER DIVE

The Price of Offshore Wind

Generally, onshore wind farms are significantly cheaper than coal power plants. However, offshore wind farms are much more expensive. Much of this cost comes from building the turbines. Turbines in the oceans need to withstand much harsher environments than those on land. Offshore turbines must be strongly anchored to the ocean floor, which can be a difficult process. Saltwater easily corrodes metal. The turbines' towers must be able to withstand constant wave action. Strong winds can bring particularly powerful waves. In some parts of the world, hurricanes and cyclones could batter the turbines.

Once the turbine is built, it is also expensive to lay underwater cables called submarine cables to bring the electricity to land. Offshore wind power is one of the most expensive systems to connect to the grid. Maintenance for offshore wind farms is also very expensive. It costs much more money to send a maintenance crew out to sea. It is also much more difficult to fix a problem if it is underwater than if it is buried underground.

Offshore wind farms cost much more to build and maintain compared to those built on land.

Currently, there are no functional offshore wind farms in North America, but many have been proposed. Some people have fought these developments because they think it will make the sea less beautiful. However, one company expects its offshore wind farm off the coast of Rhode Island to be operational by the end of 2016.

A crane is used to lift the large rotor to the top of a new wind turbine.

Old lines might need to be replaced in order to handle larger amounts of electricity.

Wind farms are also typically located in rural areas. But the places that use the most electricity are cities. New power lines sometimes must be constructed over long distances to bring power to the people who need it. According to the EIA, the cost of transmitting electricity for wind power will be almost three times higher than it is for a coal power plant. These costs are $1.20 per megawatt-hour for coal and $3.10 per megawatt-hour for wind. Overall, however, these costs are fairly small—less than 5 percent of wind's total costs.

Should Governments Support Wind Power?

One final argument for the high cost of wind energy is that governments help pay for some of it. In order to encourage developers of wind power,

We must consider many things when talking about the economics of wind power. These include cost, demand, and impacts on people, wildlife, and the environment.

some governments offer **subsidies**. A subsidy is a payment or other benefit from a government to help a particular industry. In the United States, wind developers have received grants from the US government to help build wind farms. They have also received tax credits. This means that wind farm developers didn't have to pay as much tax to the government.

For example, in 2014, the US government agreed to give three offshore wind projects up to $47 million each. Many European countries also offer subsidies to wind power. In recent years, Germany has given the most subsidies to renewable energy sources, averaging about $26 billion each year. Subsidies are directly paid for by taxpayers.

Opponents of subsidies believe governments should not favor one form of energy production over another. These people think that we should let the free market decide. If a company can produce cheap electricity, then people will buy it, regardless of how it's made. If a company's electricity is expensive, then no one will buy it.

Supporters of energy subsidies say a government's job is to support the health of the country overall. It's true wind power used to be more expensive than other power sources, but thanks to support from governments, that price has decreased. Companies have found more effective ways to make electricity from wind. Had the government not given its support, these companies might have failed. Supporters believe the government needs to protect its citizens from the negative effects of global warming. Cheap electricity from plants that burn fossil fuels isn't as important as a healthy environment.

There are several important questions that opponents of wind energy ask. They want to know if wind power is reliable. They wonder if turbines destroy a landscape's natural beauty. They are concerned that turbines kill birds and bats and that they could possibly harm humans as well. Finally, they're not convinced wind power is as inexpensive as its supporters say. What do these arguments mean for the future of wind power?

CRITICAL THINKING

- If you believe wind turbines are ugly, is that enough for you to oppose wind power?

- Why is it important to take wildlife into consideration when building turbines?

- Why are people developing offshore wind farms if they are an expensive source of power?

Many workers monitor and operate wind farms from inside nearby control rooms, making sure the turbines operate efficiently and safely.

Chapter 4

The Future of Wind Power

Some people believe strongly that wind will help power the world's future energy needs. Others attempt to prevent wind farms from being built. What is the real future of wind power?

Wind Technology Is Changing

The first industrial wind turbines were expensive and inefficient. The first wind farm in the world was built in New Hampshire in 1980. That wind farm had twenty turbines, which had a total of 0.6 megawatts of potential power. Today, a single new turbine typically has 2 megawatts of potential power or more.

Businesses and governments have invested a lot of money into improving wind turbines. Today's wind turbines are taller, stronger, and more efficient than ever. People continue to research ways to make wind turbines even better. Wind power is providing a larger amount of the world's electricity every year. People want to be sure that new turbines are the best they can be.

A DEEPER DIVE

Turbine Innovation

Some people are researching even more unusual turbines. For example, winds at high altitudes tend to be much stronger than those near the surface. Is it possible to construct a wind turbine that could fly? In 2015, the technology company Google began testing turbines mounted on a structure that looks somewhat like an airplane but flies like a kite. These "energy kites" fly up to 820 feet (250 m) high, more than twice the height of today's tallest turbines.

Tall buildings often face strong winds. For some people, it makes sense to try to capture some of that power. Recently, some new skyscrapers have had wind turbines built into them. The Bahrain World Trade Center, built in 2008, was the first skyscraper in the world to include wind turbines. It is comprised of two separate towers, with three bridges linking the two towers and a wind turbine mounted on each bridge. Since then, several other skyscrapers with turbines included have been built. People continue to research whether it's a good investment for a building to make some of its own power.

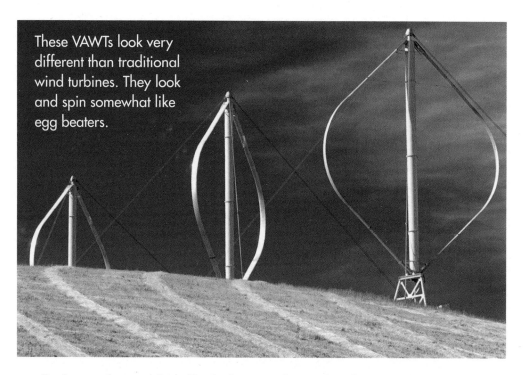

These VAWTs look very different than traditional wind turbines. They look and spin somewhat like egg beaters.

So far, we have only talked about traditional turbines. These have a rotor that points into the wind. The rotor is set atop a tall tower. These types are known as horizontal-axis wind turbines, or HAWTs. The blades spin around an imaginary horizontal line. HAWTs are by far the most common type of windmill around the world today.

However, there is a different type of turbine. The vertical-axis wind turbine, or VAWT, has curved blades that rotate around a central vertical pole. One advantage of VAWTs is that they operate regardless of wind direction. Their blades do not need to be turned into the wind like a HAWT's would. VAWTs are also easier to maintain. They are generally smaller, and they do not need tall towers to operate. A VAWT usually isn't much taller than the height of its blades. Currently, though, VAWTs aren't as efficient as HAWTs, especially for large installations. Wind farms can get more power from HAWTs. But people continue to research VAWTs to try to make them more efficient.

Small Wind

Industrial wind turbines on wind farms create power for the grid. However, some people want to live "off the grid." This means they want to make their own energy and not rely on anyone else to do it for them. Creating your own power supply is known as **microgeneration.** Using wind for microgeneration is often called "small wind."

With current technology, it is possible to have wind be the sole source of power for a home. However, the requirements are often restrictive. A turbine usually must be placed on a tower much taller than a utility pole in order to be effective. A home's location must be reviewed to ensure there is enough wind to power the turbine. Local laws might also regulate the placement of the turbine or the height of a turbine's tower, which could reduce its effectiveness.

Turbine owners must also decide what to do if the wind doesn't blow. They can choose to remain connected to the grid, and buy power when it is necessary. Or they can store wind-generated power in batteries to be completely off the grid.

A turbine that could power a home should have the ability to create at least 5 kilowatts of potential power. Although costs vary, the average cost to install such a turbine in the United States is $30,000. Federal and state governments may offer rebates and tax credits to reduce this cost. Right now, it costs a lot of money to invest in small wind, and the economic

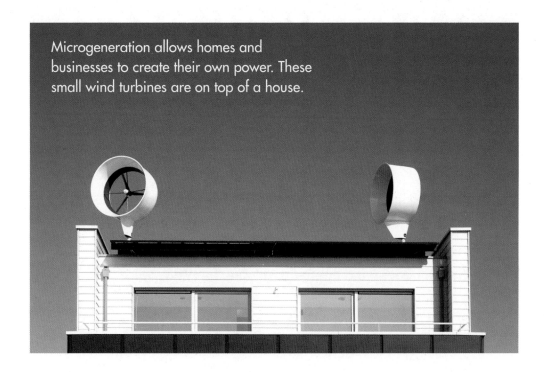
Microgeneration allows homes and businesses to create their own power. These small wind turbines are on top of a house.

value isn't always certain. Some people say that the average time to recover the cost of a home turbine is between six and thirty years. But others say those are turbine manufacturers' estimates, and the real amount of time is actually much longer.

Sustainability and the Future of Wind Power

A fundamental concept for all living things is **sustainability**. This means that all living things, including humans, depend on the natural world for survival. We must live in a way that allows the natural world to sustain us. Over the past two hundred years, humans have polluted the planet at a dangerous rate. Human activity is destroying forests, polluting the ocean, and causing

A DEEPER DIVE

Wind-Powered Schools

Iowa is a leader in wind energy. The town of Spirit Lake is located in the northwest part of the state. People there began to wonder if they could power their schools with the abundant wind energy available. In 1993, Spirit Lake built one of the first wind turbines to power a school. It provided electricity to the elementary school. The school district sold excess electricity to the local electric company, earning an additional $25,000 per year.

The loan to build the turbine was paid off in four years thanks to this additional income. Spirit Lake then built a second turbine in 2001. The turbines provide electricity for all of Spirit Lake's schools. Since 2007, Spirit Lake has earned about $120,000 per year by selling its extra power. This money is then used by the school district to help its students. The money is used to hire teachers, buy supplies, maintain athletic fields, and more.

Currently, there about two hundred elementary, middle, and high schools in the United States that own

These wind turbines in Spirit Lake, Iowa, power the town's schools. It was a revolutionary idea in 1993. Now hundreds of schools get at least a portion of their power from wind.

wind turbines. These schools use their turbines for some of their electricity needs. This microgeneration brings power costs down, which means schools can spend their money on other important things!

We are all connected on this planet. Renewable energy can help preserve the environment for people on Earth now and in the future.

global warming. Many people feel we need to radically change how we live before we completely destroy the only place we can call home.

Renewable energy sources are a large part of sustainability efforts. By using nature's power without doing further harm to the environment, we promote a sustainable future. Sustainable energy doesn't just come from wind. Solar, geothermal, and wave powers are other examples.

Renewable energy sources primarily generate electricity. But vehicles, such as cars, trucks, trains, and ships, use engines that are powered by fuels made from oil. Renewable electricity won't stop those engines from polluting. However, scientists and researchers are working towards developing effective electric engines. Several types of electric cars exist, but the distances they can travel are often limited. As time goes on, we can expect better electric engines that cost less. Part of achieving energy sustainability will be using renewable energy to charge batteries on electric vehicles. No fossil fuels will be burned. This will greatly reduce pollution and additional global warming.

It is certain wind power will have a larger role going forward. Wind power has grown rapidly in the past decade. The cost of building effective turbines has decreased a lot over the past thirty years. A single new turbine today has the potential to generate more electricity than some of the world's first wind farms. Researchers continually improve upon turbine design to capture as much of the wind's energy as possible.

In time, fossil fuels will become less and less common. This will increase their price. No one is sure how high prices need to be before people will change. In the United States, will drivers find other options to cars if gasoline costs $5 per gallon ($1.32 per liter)? What about $10 per gallon ($2.64 per liter)? All we know is that there will be a point where people will demand a cheaper mode of transportation. At the same time, as people continue to use fossil fuels, the Earth will become more polluted. Global warming will become worse.

The power of wind isn't just the ability to spin a turbine's blades. The true power of wind is that it can lead a revolution of how we think about energy. With wind power, we can have abundant, clean, safe, and cost-effective energy. Humans have used wind power for more than five thousand years. More than ever, we will rely on it as we move into the future.

CRITICAL THINKING

- Why are people experimenting with different types of turbines?

- Would you like to live in a home or building powered by small wind?

- How might solar power be better than wind power? How might it be worse?

Glossary

Coriolis effect The swirling of Earth's atmosphere because of its rotation.

dynamo A device that generates electricity using magnets and copper wire.

fossil fuels Sources of power from plants which decomposed hundreds of millions of years ago and are deeply buried. They include coal, oil, and natural gas.

global warming The recent increase of the Earth's average temperature because of human activity and pollution.

greenhouse gas A gas that is released into the atmosphere and then gets trapped there, warming the Earth like a greenhouse. Examples include carbon dioxide, methane, and fluorocarbons.

grid The system of power plants, substations, wires, and cables that delivers electricity to the general community.

kilowatt-hour (kWh) A unit that measures amounts of electricity.

levelized cost of electricity (LCOE) A standardized cost of electricity per megawatt-hour that enables price comparisons of different power sources.

megawatt-hour (MWh) One thousand kilowatt-hours.

microgeneration A home or business creating its own electricity.

millstone A large stone inside a windmill which turns and crushes grain into flour.

nacelle A box on top of a wind turbine that contains the machinery necessary to generate electricity.

nonrenewable resources Energy sources that have a limited supply, such as fossil fuels.

renewable resources Energy sources that are limitless, such as the wind, sun, and water.

rotor The blades of a windmill.

subsidies Financial support from a government to encourage a particular industry.

sustainability The idea that all living things depend on the natural world for survival and that we should therefore protect it.

vane A small tail on the back of a windmill that helps point its blades into the wind.

wind farm A collection of wind turbines in a concentrated area.

wind turbine The modern name for windmills that generate electricity.

Find Out More

Books

Morris, Neil. *Wind Power.* Energy Sources. North Mankato, MN: Smart Apple Media, 2007.

O'Neal, Claire. *How to Use Wind Power to Light and Heat Your Home.* Tell Your Parents. Hockessin, DE: Mitchell Lane Publishers, 2010.

Spilsbury, Richard and Louise. *The Pros and Cons of Wind Power.* The Energy Debate. New York: Rosen Publishing, 2008.

Walker, Niki. *Generating Wind Power.* Energy Revolution. New York: Crabtree Publishing, 2007.

Find Out More

Websites

American Wind Energy Association

www.awea.org

The AWEA is the "national trade association for the US wind industry." Its job is to convince people that wind power is a good energy source. Its website examines many issues to show why wind power is beneficial.

European Platform against Windfarms

www.epaw.org

Based in Ireland, this group wishes to stop "useless and destructive" wind farms throughout Europe. Their website features news stories and videos which argue against wind power.

European Wind Energy Association

www.ewea.org

The EWEA is similar to the AWEA above, except it focuses primarily on Europe. Most European countries have invested in wind for longer than the US has. The EWEA "raises awareness about the benefits of wind power."

National Wind Watch

www.wind-watch.org

National Wind Watch is "a coalition of groups and individuals working to save rural and wild places from heedless industrial wind energy development." They do not believe wind turbines should be built, and present arguments against them.

US Department of Energy: Wind

www.energy.gov/science-innovation/energy-sources/renewable-energy/wind

The Department of Energy's page about wind offers up-to-date news about wind power in the United States. It also includes many maps to show where and how wind power is changing the country.

US Department of Energy: WINDExchange

apps2.eere.energy.gov/wind/windexchange

WINDExchange offers statistics, maps, and information for communities interested in wind power. It includes basics about wind power as well as information about schools that use wind power across the United States.

US Environmental Protection Agency

www.epa.gov/cleanenergy/energy-and-you/affect/index.html

"How Does Electricity Affect the Environment?" allows you to select a source of power and learn how it impacts the natural world. The descriptions consider air, water, and land impacts, among other factors.

Index

Page numbers in **boldface** are illustrations. Entries in **boldface** are glossary terms.

bats, 50–51, 53, **53**, 60
birds, 50–53, **51**, 60
Brush, Charles, 12, 19–20, **21**, 22–23

California, 13, 36
Chernobyl, 40
coal, 22–23, 25, 29, 30, **31**, 38–39, **38**, 41–42, 48–49, 55–56, 58
Coriolis effect, 6, 9

Darrieus, Georges Jean Marie, 12
dynamo, 12, 19, 22, 33

electric cars, 70
Energy Information Administration, 42, 55, 58

Faraday, Michael, 12, 19

fossil fuels, 22–23, 25–26, 29–32, 35, 38–39, 53, 60, 70–71

global warming, 29, 31–32, **31**, 38–39, 53, 60, 67, 70–71
greenhouse gas, 13, 31, 38
grid, 12, 34–35, **34**, 41, 55–56, 66

infrasound, 54–55

kilowatt-hour (kWh), 34, 36, 41

levelized cost of electricity (LCOE), 41–42
London Array, 13, 36, **37**, 52

megawatt-hour (MWh), 34, 41–42, 55, 58
microgeneration, 66–69, **67**,
millstone, 14

nacelle, 32–33, **33**, 39
Netherlands, the, 10, 12, 15, **16**, 17

nonrenewable resources, 25 29
  See also coal; fossil fuels; oil
nuclear power, 38–40, 42, 49

oil, 12, 22–23, 25–26, 29–30, 70
oil crisis, 12, **24**, 25–26

renewable resources, 35, 45, 48,
  59, 70, **70**
rotor, 22, 32–33, **33**, 38, 48, 53,
  58, 65

sailing, 5–6, 9–12, **10**, 14
skyscrapers, 64
Spirit Lake, Iowa, 68–69, **69**
subsidies, 13, 58–60
sustainability, 44, 67, 70

vane, 19, 33

wind farm, 13, 35, 36, **37**, 42,
  48–49, 52, 55–59, **57**, **62**, 63,
  66, 71

windmills, 5, 12, 14–15, **16**, 17–
  20, **18**, **21**, 22–23, 32
wind power
  advantages of, 35, 38–39,
    41–42, 47, 49, 70–71
  disadvantages of, 45–46, 48–51,
    50, **51**, 53–58, 60, 66–67
  explanation of wind, 5–9, **7**
  history, 9–15, **10**, 17–20, **18**,
    21, 22–23, 26
  how it works, 32–34, **33**
wind turbines
  animals and, 50–53, **51**, **53**
  construction of, 35, 41, **42**, 50,
    50, 55–56, **58**, 68
  design of, **28**, 32–33, **33**, 41,
    48, 63–66, 71
  generating electricity, 5, 12,
    33–35, 41, 45–46, 55, 63,
    66, **67**, 68–69, **69**, 71
  location of, 35, 48, 53–54, 56, 66
  safety of, 39, **39**, 41, 53–55,
    54, **62**
  VAWTs, 12, 65–66, **65**

About the Author

B. J. Best grew up with the wind by learning how to sail on a small lake in Wisconsin. He still lives there, near some of the largest wind farms in the state. He has published two other books with Cavendish Square and teaches English and writing at Carroll University. He would like to have his own wind turbine someday.